The heavily wooded Edgewood Tahoe Golf Club makes its home on the site of a former cattle ranch in Stateline, Nevada. One family has owned the ranch-turned-golf-course for generations, and the family ranch house, which served at various times as an inn and a Pony Express station, still stands near the course. This course is as tough as the cowboys who once roamed it. The lake, pond, and streams bring water into play on twelve holes, and the large, slick greens that often lead to three-putts are protected by numerous rugged sand traps. Fortunately, this rigorous golf course is set against beautiful Lake Tahoe with the breathtaking Sierra Nevadas as a backdrop—a sight that soothes the nerves of frustrated golfers.

Date _____ August 15, 1995

Score _____ 84 (with 2 birdies!)

Partners _____ Debbie and Steve + Jan Adams

Notes _____ Beautiful course! Watch out for trees - especially on 16, a par 5 with 2 killer fairway bunkers (bogeyed that one). Be sure to call Steve + Jan next time in town (702-555-1245) and have dinner on Tahoe Queen.

A Golfer's Travel Journal

Cover photo: Mahogany Run's 14th hole

Published by Taylor Publishing Company
1550 West Mockingbird Lane
Dallas, Texas 75235

Printed in the United States of America

10   9   8   7   6   5   4   3   2   1

A Golfer's
TRAVEL
JOURNAL

TAYLOR PUBLISHING COMPANY

Dallas, Texas

Amana Colonies

*A*mana Colonies Golf Course has a unique history that dates back to the formation of the Community of True Inspiration in Germany in 1714. The Community immigrated to America and eventually founded the village of Amana on the Iowa River in 1854. The people lived communally until 1932 when they incorporated their holdings and formed the Amana Society. Amana Colonies is laid out on land that has been leased from the Amana Society for over one hundred years. This extraordinary golf course is as unique as its heritage. Each hole has been literally sculpted out of a dense forest and has a look and feel all its own. Elevations vary throughout the rolling course, and ponds, creeks, and ravines are quick to consume stray golf balls. A round of golf at Amana Colonies allows you to immerse yourself in the splendor of a woodland world.

Date _____

Score _____

Partners _____

Notes _____

_____

_____

_____

_____

_____

_____

Anchorage

*A*laska is famed for its wilderness adventures such as bear hunting, ice fishing, and even dog sledding, so you might be surprised to discover a top-flight golf course on the outskirts of one of its busiest seaports. Anchorage Golf Course, set snuggly in foothills of the Chugach Mountains, is an outdoor adventure of its own. Its tight fairways and small greens are surrounded by rugged Alaskan woods, thick with native spruce and white birch. The sparkling lakes that come into play reflect the pristine beauty of this virgin wilderness and add a considerable degree of difficulty to this testy course. On a crisp, clear day, you can see as far as Mt. McKinley, a fitting view from this monumental golf course.

Date _____

Score _____

Partners _____

Notes _____

_____

_____

_____

_____

_____

_____

_____

Bent Creek

*I*nspired by the splendor of the Great Smoky Mountains, Gary Player designed one of his first courses at Bent Creek Golf Resort. A brilliant array of flora and fauna enliven this wooded Tennessee course. Bent Creek's front nine is couched in the valley, while its back nine is a typical mountain layout. One of the course's major hazards is Bent Creek itself, which combines with other aquatic hazards to bring water into play on thirteen holes. But take care not to spend too much time concentrating on your game or you'll miss out on the awesome Smoky Mountain vistas that backdrop this outstanding course.

Date _____

Score _____

Partners _____

Notes _____

_____

_____

_____

_____

_____

_____

_____

_____

_____

_____

The Bluffs

*T*he Bluffs on Thompson Creek just north of Baton Rouge captures the mysterious allure of the Feliciana Wilderness, which was discovered by John James Audubon when he painted his "Birds of America" series. Gracing plantation land that dates back to the 1700s, the Bluffs' contoured fairways are carved from thick woodlands of mature hardwoods and pines. They feature extreme elevation changes and end at large, undulating greens, and their steep slopes are made even more difficult with tons of sand and water on seventeen holes, giving it the highest slope rating from the Championship tees in Louisiana. This woodland golf course, a virtual wildlife sanctuary, will delight you at every turn.

Date _____

Score _____

Partners _____

Notes _____

_____

_____

_____

_____

_____

_____

_____

Breckenridge

*B*reckenridge Golf Club claims the distinction of being the only Jack Nicklaus-designed municipal course in existence. At an altitude of 9,300 feet, this open course offers spectacular panoramas of four mountain ranges, including the Rockies. Although Breckenridge is predominantly a mountain-style course that winds up and down valleys with streams meandering throughout, lush green forests and swampy wetland areas add to the character of this alluring golf arena. The natural hazards created by this diverse setting along with the water that comes into play on more than half the holes make Breckenridge a formidable challenge.

Date _____

Score _____

Partners _____

Notes _____

_____

_____

_____

_____

_____

_____

_____

_____

_____

_____

Cacapon

*C*acapon Mountain calmly surveys the sprawling six thousand acres of Cacapon Resort State Park stretched out below it in Berkeley Springs. Nestled within this wooded West Virginia park is a graceful golf course accented by gentle hills and sparkling water. Deer and other creatures of the forest often wander onto the course, making quiet appearances before scurrying back to their woodland homes. Everything about Cacapon lends itself to a carefree atmosphere, and its pleasantly challenging course perfectly blends relaxing golf and a refreshing taste of nature.

Date _____

Score _____

Partners _____

Notes _____

_____

_____

_____

_____

_____

_____

_____

_____

_____

Castle Harbour

*L*ocated in Tucker's Town, Bermuda, Castle Harbour Golf Club offers a total golfing experience. Opened in 1931, this spectacular course was originally designed by Charles Banks and later redesigned by Robert Trent Jones. Castle Habour's lustrious seaside setting is pleasing to the eye but can mean trouble for your golf game. Its steep hills often provide precarious lies and send putts rolling toward the ocean, whose mighty winds blow across the lush fairways and carefully manicured greens. With majestic views of the turquoise ocean, bright coral reefs, and pink oleander and hibiscus coloring the course, Castle Harbour is sure to test your game and delight your senses.

Date _____

Score _____

Partners _____

Notes _____

_____

_____

_____

_____

_____

_____

_____

_____

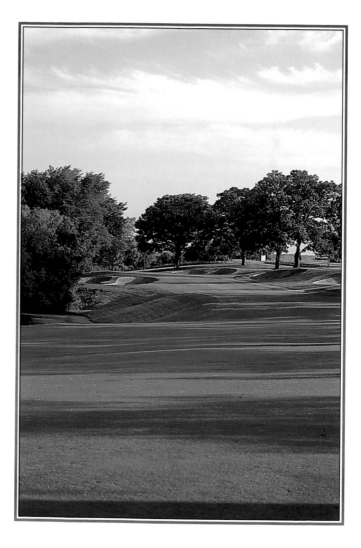

Cog Hill

*F*our outstanding eighteen-hole courses grace Cog Hill Golf and Country Club located just outside of Chicago. The first member of this fabulous foursome was built in 1926 by Bert F. Coghill and Dave McIntosh, and the last, Dubsdread, was completed in 1964. The youngest course is the most well known of the harmonious quartet. It's a traditional-style course that doesn't harbor any hidden hazards, but those that you see are difficult enough—especially when you factor in the quick greens and narrow fairways. The other three courses at Cog Hill are a more moderate challenge—with mature trees, water hazards, and plenty of sand—but not deadly. The symphony of courses at Cog Hill are music to the ears of any golfer.

Date _____

Score _____

Partners _____

Notes _____

_____

_____

_____

_____

_____

_____

_____

Concord

*S*et in the foothills of the Catskill Mountains, Concord Championship Golf Club harbors a frightening beast of a course— The Monster. Although the club houses a kinder, gentler course—the International—with rolling hills, few water hazards, and less yardage, it's The Monster's amazing rigor that has earned Concord renown. Practically flooded with lakes, streams, and ponds, this menacing course boasts ten water hazards that bring water into play on almost every hole. In addition to its exhausting length and abundant water, fairway bunkers are placed treacherously throughout. Lurking among the tall pines and wooded mountains of the Catskills is the golf adventure of a lifetime.

Date _____

Score _____

Partners _____

Notes _____

_____

_____

_____

_____

_____

_____

_____

_____

Coeur d'Alene

*R*anked among the five most beautiful lakes in the world, Lake Coeur d'Alene in northern Idaho makes a gorgeous site for a golf course. Coeur d'Alene Resort Golf Course features lake views from holes one through eighteen, but it's most famous hole is fourteen, which boasts an island green that is actually a 15,000-foot floating pontoon. Reachable only by boat, the green comes complete with its own trees, flowers, bunkers, and water recycling system. But Coeur d'Alene is not as gimmicky as it may sound. In addition to its stunning lake vista backdropped by densely wooded slopes, the course also emphasizes natural features such as forests, Fernan Creek, sandy lakeshores, and rolling terrain. Aesthetically pleasing and mentally challenging, Coeur d'Alene is a course well worth experiencing.

Date _____

Score _____

Partners _____

Notes _____

_____

_____

_____

_____

_____

_____

_____

Deer Creek

*L*ocated in the prosperous Overland Park suburb, Deer Creek Golf Club has reason to be proud of its fifteenth hole. Voted the most difficult hole in Kansas City, it is better known as "Devastation." This par three starts off of an elevated tee, usually taking you into the wind, and ends at a narrow bentgrass green fortified by bunkers on either side and a stream crossing in front. The other seventeen holes at Deer Creek are no cakewalk either, with eighty-five bunkers strategically placed throughout the course and water on thirteen holes. The wooded Kansas setting lines the fairways with oak, hickory, maple, ash, and sycamore, and Midwestern critters such as deer, quail, fox, geese bring the scene to life.

Date _____

Score _____

Partners _____

Notes _____

_____

_____

_____

_____

_____

_____

_____

_____

Dogwood Hills

*D*ogwood Hills Golf Course marries the down-home charm of its Missouri setting with the understated elegance of a premier golf course. Nestled in the gently rolling, thickly wooded Ozark Mountains, this rustic course captures the true spirit of the historic hills that embrace it. Although the generous fairways and undulating greens can be tricky at times, they generally make for a friendly round of golf. The brilliant Lake of the Ozarks shines beneath surrounding mountain foliage at Dogwood Hills, inviting you to kick back and enjoy your game.

Date _____

Score _____

Partners _____

Notes _____

_____

_____

_____

_____

_____

_____

_____

_____

_____

_____

Eagle Bend

*A*lthough fairly new to the golf world, Eagle Bend Golf Club quickly received acclaim as one of Montana's top public courses. The quaint community of Bigfork, located in the floor of the Flathead River Valley, is a picturesque setting for this superb golf course. Both Flathead Lake and Flathead River wet this rolling course, making water a constant hindrance. The generous greens are difficult to reach because they are well guarded by sand traps and, of course, more water. With the Mission Mountains in the distance, the river meandering through the course, and the moose and deer that watch from the woods, Eagle Bend embodies the spirit of the Montana heartland.

Date _____

Score _____

Partners _____

Notes _____

_____

_____

_____

_____

_____

_____

_____

_____

Edgewood Tahoe

*T*he heavily wooded Edgewood Tahoe Golf Club makes its home on the site of a former cattle ranch in Stateline, Nevada. One family has owned the ranch-turned-golf-course for generations, and the family ranch house, which served at various times as an inn and a Pony Express station, still stands near the course. This course is as tough as the cowboys who once roamed it. The lake, pond, and streams bring water into play on twelve holes, and the large, slick greens that often lead to three-putts are protected by numerous rugged sand traps. Fortunately, this rigorous golf course is set against beautiful Lake Tahoe with the breathtaking Sierra Nevadas as a backdrop—a sight that soothes the nerves of frustrated golfers.

Date _____

Score _____

Partners _____

Notes _____

_____

_____

_____

_____

_____

_____

_____

Emerald Valley

*T*he majestic Cascade Mountains are an impressive backdrop for Emerald Valley Golf Course, which can be found just south of Eugene, Oregon. Laid out along the Willamette River in the rolling foothills beneath the mountains, Emerald Valley will challenge the abilities of any golfer. Its heavily wooded setting makes trees a common hazard and creates tight fairways. The winding river and three ponds that dot the course increase its difficulty and add to the natural splendor of the valley. With deep green trees and crisp mountain air, this lush valley and its beautiful course are as precious as their name.

Date _____

Score _____

Partners _____

Notes _____

_____

_____

_____

_____

_____

_____

_____

_____

Farm Neck

*L*ocated on charming Martha's Vineyard, Farm Neck Golf Club is an ideal golf getaway. Its gently rolling layout provides splendrous vistas of the cool blue ocean, whose waves softly lap against the coastline. Farm Neck's narrow front nine sports numerous sand traps and is slightly more demanding than its longer but more open back nine. Perhaps the most difficult hazards to avoid are the saucy seagulls that are known to carry away unattended golf balls. In fact, Farm Neck has a house rule that "any ball moved or stolen by seagulls should be moved back or played at the original lie." The soothing setting of this peaceful golf course offers a relaxing escape from the toil of daily life.

Date _____

Score _____

Partners _____

Notes _____

_____

_____

_____

_____

_____

_____

_____

_____

Firethorn

*F*irethorn Golf Club in Lincoln, Nebraska, sports a traditional links-style design. Designed by Pete Dye, it features mildly undulating fairways, railroad ties around the sparse water hazards, and native grasses enclosing the fairways. These tall grasses are perhaps the most formidable hazard at Firethorn—a ball hit into them is almost certainly lost. This Midwestern course's unique signature is number seventeen, which was originally to be modeled after the seventeenth at TPC at Sawgrass with its famous island green. In the end, however, it turned out to be a semi-island green with water surrounding almost half of it. Named for a large, wicked shrub with barbed needles, Firethorn is as dangerous as its namesake.

Date _____

Score _____

Partners _____

Notes _____

_____

_____

_____

_____

_____

_____

_____

Four Seasons

he TPC Course at the Four Seasons Resort and Club in Irving (between Dallas and Fort Worth) is tailored for the thinking golfer. This demanding course is not particularly long and its crafted layout requires more finesse than power. A creek winds through the narrow fairways, coming into play on nine holes, and the slick greens are well-guarded by cavernous bunkers. Tricky winds are also a common irritation, as professionals such as Craig Stadler, Ben Crenshaw, and Ernie Els have discovered while playing in the annual GTE Byron Nelson Classic. Even these golf greats have to put their thinking caps on to maneuver through the Four Seasons.

Date _____

Score _____

Partners _____

Notes _____

_____

_____

_____

_____

_____

_____

_____

_____

French Lick

*I*ndiana's French Lick Springs Resort can accommodate a friendly round for the laid-back golfer or a rigorous trial for the thrill seeker. It offers two traditional courses: the mild-mannered Valley Course and the unforgiving Country Club Course. Featuring only a handful of sand traps and two harmless brooks, the Valley Course invites golfers seeking a relaxing afternoon. Country Club, on the other hand, is a ferocious course that creeps over wooded hills and steals stray balls with its deep bunkers. So, whether your golfing style is fearless or fearful, French Lick has a course for you.

Date _____

Score _____

Partners _____

Notes _____

_____

_____

_____

_____

_____

_____

_____

_____

_____

Glen Oak

*G*olfers of every level will enjoy a challenging round of golf on traditional Glen Oak Golf Course in Amherst, New York. The course's flat fairways are deceptively difficult because of their strategically placed bunkers and Black Creek snaking its way into play on fifteen holes. Woods dense with mature trees line the fairways, leaving little room for error. And mischievous forest dwellers scamper about Glen Oak unchecked, often wandering onto the course from the woods or creek bed to add a little excitement to an otherwise peaceful round of golf. That's why regulars often refer to the course as "The Game Farm."

Date _____

Score _____

Partners _____

Notes _____

_____

_____

_____

_____

_____

_____

_____

_____

Grand Traverse

*T*outed as one of the top golf spots in Michigan, Grand Traverse Resort is located just a few miles outside of Traverse City, not far from the coast of Lake Huron. It features two outstanding courses: The Bear Course and Spruce Run Course. As you may have guessed, The Bear is named for its creator, Jack Nicklaus. Tearing through hardwood forests and orchards, it is as ferocious as it sounds. Spruce Run, although less difficult than The Bear, presents challenges of its own. The wind often sweeps through its open expanses, making accurate shots a difficult task, and the twelve water hazards are always ready to swallow a ball that has been blown off course. Both Grand Traverse courses offer superb golfing experiences.

Date _____

Score _____

Partners _____

Notes _____

_____

_____

_____

_____

_____

_____

_____

Great Sand Dunes

*G*reat Sand Dunes Country Club in Mosca is truly a home where the buffalo roam and the deer and the antelope play. Cradled in the San Luis Valley, this rustic golf course incorporates desert features into a Scottish-links-style layout. The course rambles through aromatic fields of sage and buffalo grass with mountain-fed streams and ponds coming into play on six holes. Fantastic overlooks are awaiting in every direction, from the Great Sand Dunes National Monument to the snowcapped peaks of the San Juan Mountain Range to the third largest buffalo herd in America. Located at Colorado's historic Zapata Ranch, Great Sand Dunes is a tranquil world where seldom is heard a discouraging word and the skies are not cloudy all day.

Date _____

Score _____

Partners _____

Notes _____

_____

_____

_____

_____

_____

_____

_____

Half Moon

*S*ituated in the tropical paradise of Montego Bay, Half Moon Golf Club can't be far from Eden. Bougainvillea, hibiscus, and oleanders flourish on the rich green fairways, which are lined with palm, willow, rubber, and coconut trees that sway in the ocean breeze. Even the more than one hundred sand traps are attractive, each varying in shape and size and strategically placed throughout the course. With its winning combination of beauty and challenge, it's easy to see why Half Moon is the celebrated site of the Jamaican Open.

Date _____

Score _____

Partners _____

Notes _____

_____

_____

_____

_____

_____

_____

_____

_____

_____

_____

Hidden Valley

*P*oised atop a three thousand-foot peak, Hidden Valley Resort Golf Course offers thirty-mile vistas of the wooded Pennsylvania mountains that surround it. This rolling course is chiseled out of a dense hardwood forest, and its narrow, tree-lined fairways place a premium on accuracy. Running along natural fall lines rather than the traditional parallel layout, each hole at Hidden Valley is a unique experience. In every season, Mother Nature dazzles your senses and tests your mettle with water, sand, and rock outcroppings scattered about this tedious course. Offering all you could want in mountaintop golf, Hidden Valley Resort is unsurpassed in its beauty and charm.

Date _____

Score _____

Partners _____

Notes _____

_____

_____

_____

_____

_____

_____

_____

_____

Hilton Head National

*O*f the more than twenty courses on Hilton Head Island off the South Carolina coast, Hilton Head National Golf Club ranks among the best. The fairways stretch out virtually uninterrupted, and their major hazards are the tall grass and knobby mounds that creep along their edges. This open layout gives it the feel of a genuine links course while serving up a generous portion of Southern coastal landscape with dense woods surrounding some fairways and natural marshlands bordering others. The combination of links design and natural terrain is sure to challenge the finest golfer. And be sure to watch out for the love grass—it's not as sweet as it sounds when it swallows your ball.

Date _____

Score _____

Partners _____

Notes _____

_____

_____

_____

_____

_____

_____

_____

Horseshoe Bay

*L*ocated in the heart of Texas Hill Country, Horseshoe Bay Country Club Resort features three unique yet complimentary golf courses: Slick Rock, Applerock, and Ramrock. This Robert Trent Jones trilogy is laid out through green valleys wooded with cedar, mesquite, and persimmon and studded by granite outcroppings. In addition to other water hazards, the Slick Rock Course boasts the club's signature hole, number fourteen, which is traversed by an enormous tumbling waterfall. Steep hills, eight water holes, and narrow fairways contribute to Ramrock's reputation as one of the most difficult courses in Texas. Stunning lake LBJ can be viewed from the hills of the Applerock course. Perhaps the most scenic of the three courses, it also features streams, spring-fed creeks, and ravines. This medley of courses create a magnificent harmony with Horseshoe Bay's own natural surroundings.

Date _____

Score _____

Partners _____

Notes _____

_____

_____

_____

_____

Indian Canyon

*D*esigned by U.S. Amateur Champion Chandler Egan in 1935, Indian Canyon Golf Course in Spokane, Washington, is an enchanting spot for golf. Its Pacific Northwest terrain is heavily wooded with large old pine and fur trees that tighten its hilly fairways. The city of Spokane, which is named after a Native American word meaning "children of the sun," and the valley below stretch out before you from the first and tenth holes. Like most holes on this verdant course, these two are dry but made difficult by uneven fairways and ill-placed trees. From its hilltop tees to its tiny greens, Indian Canyon is a bumpy ride.

Date _____

Score _____

Partners _____

Notes _____

_____

_____

_____

_____

_____

_____

_____

_____

_____

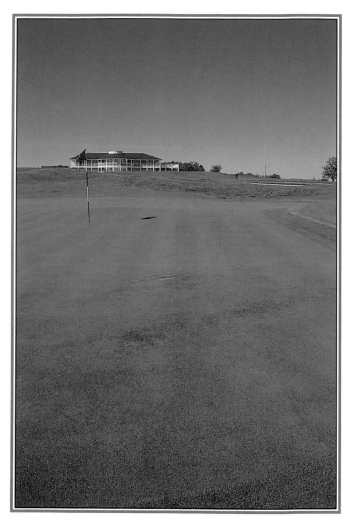

Kearney Hill

*K*earney Hill Golf Links finds itself fenced in the surrounding horse farms that populate the Kentucky countryside. You won't see any ponies on this course, but long par fours are a sure bet. These tough holes are made even harder by the traditional pot bunkers and minihills of a links-style course. An unexpected feature of Kearney Hill's open course is bentgrass greens and fairways, which are a rare find in this neck of the woods. Traditional in layout and unique in atmosphere, Kearney Hill is one of the hidden treasures of the South.

Date _____

Score _____

Partners _____

Notes _____

_____

_____

_____

_____

_____

_____

_____

_____

_____

_____

Ko Olina

*B*asking on the sunny western shore of Oahu, Ko Olina Golf Club sports an exceptional championship golf course. In addition to the dangers of the Hawaiian coastline, this waterlogged course is made difficult by blue lakes, lively streams, and rushing waterfalls that come into play on eight holes. The sweeping kona winds that blow in off the Pacific won't help you steer clear of these thirsty hazards either. Between the exotic location and the challenging natural hazards, it's easy to see why Ko Olina is frequently selected to stage so many professional tournaments.

Date _____

Score _____

Partners _____

Notes _____

_____

_____

_____

_____

_____

_____

_____

_____

_____

Lakewood

*L*ocated on the Point Clear peninsula in Point Clear, Alabama, the Lakewood Golf Club features two traditional golf courses. The back nine of the Dogwood Course is considered the toughest at Lakewood, but the Azalea Course boasts the club's signature hole, the par-5 fourteenth. Trees lined along on the right side and sand traps stretching down the left tighten the fairway that ends at an island green. Lakewood's many lagoons mirror its great old oaks that drip with Spanish moss and remind you that you are indeed in the Heart of Dixie.

Date _____

Score _____

Partners _____

Notes _____

_____

_____

_____

_____

_____

_____

_____

_____

_____

_____

Legends

One of the most exciting golf complexes of the Grand Strand is The Legends Golf Club in Myrtle Beach. Its six outstanding courses vary from flat, traditional links to wooded and winding. Two of the courses, Heathland and Moorland are reminiscent of Scotland's ancient courses with their undulating dunes, sod-walled bunkers, treeless land, and vast waste areas. The rolling fairways of Parkland and Heritage Club's century-old oaks and magnolias contrast dramatically with these links-style courses. The Legends also features Marsh Harbour, outlined by salt marshes and natural vegetation, and Oyster Bay. Trademark oyster shells and oyster walls accent Oyster Bay's innovative holes, including its two island greens. The formidable layouts and spellbinding scenery of The Legends create a premier golf experience.

Date _____

Score _____

Partners _____

Notes _____

_____

_____

_____

_____

_____

_____

_____

Lely Flamingo Island

*T*he Gulf of Mexico's bright blue waters meet sandy white beaches at the Lely Flamingo Island Club. Sable palms, palmettos, cypress, and other exotic plants enrich this golf gem. Rolling past thirsty lagoons and around funky, free-form bunkers, its fairways, although typically wide, are a treacherous trip for any golf ball. With water coming into play on thirteen holes and cool breezes blowing in off the Gulf, Lely Flamingo Island Club will lure you in with its tropical beauty only to terrorize your golf game.

Date _____

Score _____

Partners _____

Notes _____

_____

_____

_____

_____

_____

_____

_____

_____

_____

Lyman Orchards

*T*he land of Lyman Orchards Golf Club in Middle-field, Connecticut, has been in the Lyman family since John Lyman purchased the original thirty acres in 1741. The history-rich club features two champion-ship courses: one designed by Robert Trent Jones in 1969 and the other by Gary Player in 1994. The rolling, tree-lined fair-ways of the Jones course's back nine are traditional, traveling over and around water on seven holes. The younger Player design features fairways that are far more demanding than its elder—accuracy is a must, deep ravines are a constant threat, and several holes weave around ponds. Luckily, the greens are flat and true. Farms, meadows, orchards, and hills surrounding this New England course add to its alluring charm.

Date _____

Score _____

Partners _____

Notes _____

_____

_____

_____

_____

_____

_____

_____

Mahogany Run

*T*his spectacular course is located on the northern shore of St. Thomas. Rising and dropping along the coastline of cliffs with crashing blue sea below, Mahogany Run Golf Club is breathtaking in every sense of the word. The tumultuous course is a roller-coaster ride through dense, lush rain forest that ends at Devil's Triangle. This aptly named part of the course is made up of the 13th, 14th, and 15th holes, each balanced on the carved edge of a cliff. They demand carries over dizzying drops that are certain death for a muffed shot. These and other thrilling features make Mahogany Run the ultimate golfing adventure.

Date _____

Score _____

Partners _____

Notes _____

_____

_____

_____

_____

_____

_____

_____

_____

Majestic Oaks

*S*ettled just northwest of Minneapolis in Ham Lake, Majestic Oaks Country Club boasts two precious golf courses—Platinum and Gold. The Platinum is the more challenging of the two. Its woodland areas, marshy lowlands, and numerous water hazards are death to errant golf balls. On the brighter side, they also bring the course to life with deer, fox, geese, and other native wildlife. The flatter, shorter Gold Course is somewhat easier than the Platinum, but with its narrow fairways, ponds, and swamplands it's no walk in the park. Although they vary in difficulty, both Majestic Oaks courses are equally magnificent in beauty.

Date _____

Score _____

Partners _____

Notes _____

_____

_____

_____

_____

_____

_____

_____

_____

Makena

*T*he exotic surroundings of Makena Golf Course create a golf paradise. Breathtaking views are offered in every direction, from the ocean to the mountains to the Haleakala Crater. Robert Trent Jones Jr. left nature and history untouched when he laid out the 36 holes of the North and South Courses. Original Hawaiian rock walls remain where they were found, gullies and stream beds have been left unaltered, and Makena's indigenous kiawe trees still stand where they took root centuries ago. A day on this beautiful course gives you a true sense of the mana (the Hawaiian word for "spirit of the land") of Makena.

Date _____

Score _____

Partners _____

Notes _____

_____

_____

_____

_____

_____

_____

_____

_____

Meadowbrook

*L*aid out on the flood plain of Rapid Creek, Meadowbrook Golf Club has been rated as the best public course in South Dakota. This elegant course lies only twelve miles from Mount Rushmore and provides a stunning view of the Black Hills. Its variety of native trees—weeping birch, black walnut, elm, poplar, cottonwood, and pine are just a few—give it a unique charm. With over one hundred sand traps and Rapid Creek coming into play on nine holes, Meadowbrook is a true test for any golfer.

Date _____

Score _____

Partners _____

Notes _____

_____

_____

_____

_____

_____

_____

_____

_____

_____

Minot

Minot Country Club bears distinction, possessing one of the oldest golf courses in North Dakota. Founded as a nine-hole course in the 1920s, Minot added a back nine in the early 1950s to form one of the finest courses in the state. Its understated layout spreads out over generally flat terrain sprinkled with towering evergreens. Containing few sand traps and even fewer water hazards, Minot doesn't tease with tricky holes or hidden gimmicks; even the bentgrass greens are what they seem—small and quick. The uncluttered setting and fresh country air make Minot a good walking course and a pleasure to play.

Date _____

Score _____

Partners _____

Notes _____

_____

_____

_____

_____

_____

_____

_____

_____

_____

Montaup

*S*ituated a few miles northeast of Newport, Montaup Country Club is set against serene Mt. Hope Bay. Its sixteenth hole, which overlooks the quiet bay and the suspended Mt. Hope Bridge, has been called the most scenic in New England. In contrast, its starting hole, a long par four with water edging two sides of the green, is reputed to be one of the most difficult in Rhode Island. Although the pristine bay sets a magnificent stage for golf, its fickle winds make club selection the ultimate challenge at Montaup.

Date _____

Score _____

Partners _____

Notes _____

_____

_____

_____

_____

_____

_____

_____

_____

_____

_____

_____

Mountain Ranch

*R*ated the number-one public golf course in Arkansas, Mountain Ranch Golf Club in Fairfield Bay is a stern test. The mild slopes of its gentle front nine are only a warm-up for its demanding back nine, which requires precision to navigate. This true mountain course offers year-round golf with bermuda fairways thriving in the summers and rye toughing out the winter. With creative shot-making a must and splendid views of the Ozarks stretching in all directions, Mountain Ranch is a challenge and a charm.

Date _____

Score _____

Partners _____

Notes _____

_____

_____

_____

_____

_____

_____

_____

_____

_____

_____

Ojai Valley Inn

The mountain-ringed Ojai Valley in California is an enchanting setting for golf. Situated snugly at the bottom of the vast Los Padres National Forest in the Topa Topa Mountains, Ojai Valley Inn and Country Club is a Spanish-style resort. The golf course ranges from dense woods with great oaks looming over the fairways to steep hills, and arroyos run across the course, nabbing stray golf balls. Ojai is a Chumash Indian word that possibly means "the moon" or "the mist," but locals prefer to refer to their cozy habitat as "The Nest." A.D.S. Johnston said of the course, in *The Country Club*, when it first opened in 1923, "Every tee, every fairway and every green offers a different panorama, all of them beautiful. Every hole has character and individuality."

Date _____

Score _____

Partners _____

Notes _____

_____

_____

_____

_____

_____

_____

_____

Old Landing

*T*he rippling waters of Rehoboth Bay and Arnell Creek dance along the edges of Old Landing Golf Course in Rehoboth Beach. Although the bay and creek are prominent highlights of this superb course's atmosphere, they don't come into play. However, other water hazards factor in on seven holes. Hundreds of willows billow over Old Landing's relatively flat fairways. Its back nine is more heavily treed than its front, featuring four holes sculpted out of deep Delaware woods. With the cool air breezing in off the bay and osprey circling lazily overhead, Old Landing is an inviting spot for a relaxing round of golf.

Date _____

Score _____

Partners _____

Notes _____

_____

_____

_____

_____

_____

_____

_____

_____

_____

_____

PGA National

*T*he five championship courses of PGA National Golf Club offer a wide range of golf experiences. In 1990 Jack Nicklaus redesigned the Champion Course. He decreased its difficulty, but watch out because water comes into play on almost every hole. The Haig Course can also make for a wet game, winding around fifteen water hazards. If you're looking for a links–style course, look to the Squire, the shortest and narrowest of the group. Arnold Palmer designed a Scottish-style course, The General, complete with grass bunkers and a double green. The luscious Estate Course is graced with Florida pines and tropical vegetation, but its eighty-six bunkers and seventeen water hazards keep you on your toes. The country club atmosphere and Palm Beach setting of PGA National are sure to please everyone from the occasional golfer to the scratch handicapper.

Date _____

Score _____

Partners _____

Notes _____

_____

_____

_____

_____

_____

_____

PGA West,
TPC *Stadium Course*

*W*hen Pete Dye received the dictum to design the toughest course in world, he took it seriously. Only the truly brave tackle the treacherous TPC Stadium Course in La Quinta, California. Its eight lakes, covering thirty-five acres, have sent hundreds of golf balls to a watery death, and its ferocious bunkers are the most photographed in the world. The target layout of the Stadium Course and its quick greens add to the challenge. With the awesome Santa Rosa Mountains as a backdrop, you have to experience this amazing golf course to believe it.

Date _____

Score _____

Partners _____

Notes _____

_____

_____

_____

_____

_____

_____

_____

_____

_____

Palmas Del Mar

*L*aid out on an old sugar plantation, Palmas del Mar enjoys the lush green mountains of Puerto Rico on one side and the aquamarine waters of the Caribbean on the other. The narrow fairways and small greens of this course's front nine wind through endless coconut groves, while its back nine rolls over a hill that affords stunning views of the sparkling sea and El Yunque, an adjacent rain forest. The more than three thousand coconut palms that sway over this remarkable course inspired its name and add to its exotic ambience. With its challenging layout and sumptuous sights, Palmas del Mar is as sweet as is sounds.

Date _____

Score _____

Partners _____

Notes _____

_____

_____

_____

_____

_____

_____

_____

_____

Paradise Island

*E*xceeding the grandeur of its name, Paradise Island Golf Club is the premier course in the Bahamas. Located in the capital city of Nassau, Paradise Island is more than a spectacular golf course. It is also flaunts a striking bird sanctuary and a wondrous garden with bougainvillea, hibiscus, and oleanders splashing its rich green setting with vibrant color. The sparkling waters of the Gulf of Mexico border many of the rolling fairways, creating hazards to be wary of. The ficus and Australian pines dotting along the fairways add to the tropical feel of this course—especially on number six, which is set on a coral reef. Paradise Island is an exotic world of its own.

Date _____

Score _____

Partners _____

Notes _____

_____

_____

_____

_____

_____

_____

_____

_____

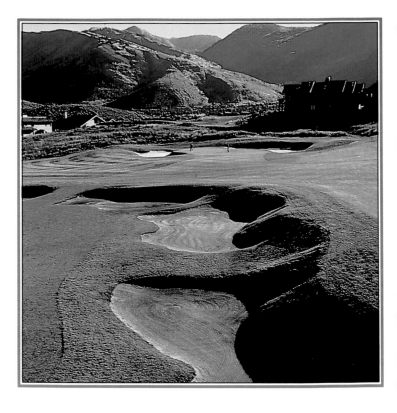

Park Meadows

*P*ark City, Utah, may be best known for its skiing, but it is also home to a premier golf course. Although Park Meadows Golf Club is relatively flat, it provides a ride as exhilarating as the slopes. Instead of moguls, it tests you with over one hundred sand traps scattered across its fairways and around its greens. There are no trees on this links-style course, sharply contrasting with the nearby wooded ski runs. But, with its deep and dangerous rough always a threat, you still have to keep your ball in the fairway. Numerous glassy lakes and meandering streams spanned by arching wooden bridges bring water into play on over half of the holes on this subtly demanding course. With its tricky bunkers, tough rough, and treacherous water hazards, Park Meadows is definitely a double diamond.

Date _____

Score _____

Partners _____

Notes _____

_____

_____

_____

_____

_____

_____

_____

Pebble Beach

*L*ong renowned as the finest and most demanding golf course in the country, Pebble Beach Golf Links became the first true links course in U.S. when it opened in 1919. This serendipitous meeting of land and water is located on the Monterey Peninsula in Carmel Bay. The Pacific Ocean makes its ominous presence known by carving its way into otherwise undisturbed stretches of fairway and using its mighty winds to send balls sailing in exactly the wrong direction. The foaming white water crashing furiously against the ragged rock beach sets the tone for Pebble Beach's deadly golf course.

Date _____

Score _____

Partners _____

Notes _____

_____

_____

_____

_____

_____

_____

_____

_____

Pine Island

*P*ine Island Golf Club stretches across three small islands in the gulf's warm waters near Ocean Springs. The variety of wildlife that abounds in Mississippi's woods and marshlands makes this golf course as appealing to nature lovers as it is to golfers. In fact, the Audubon Society occasionally visits this area to conduct research on its native animals. Pine Island's peaceful atmosphere invites you to relax, but its demanding course will keep you alert. The lakes and marshland common throughout the course make water a threat on every hole, and treks through mature trees only increase its difficulty. Pine Island's serene Southern setting is ideal for a leisurely yet challenging round of golf.

Date _____

Score _____

Partners _____

Notes _____

_____

_____

_____

_____

_____

_____

_____

_____

_____

Pine Needles

*J*ust as its name suggests, Pine Needles Resort winds its way through avenues of tall pine trees. This cozy course flows over the rolling North Carolina sandhills near Pinehurst and is as traditional in its layout as in its golf history. The esteemed Donald Ross designed this strategic course in 1927, and it is now the domain of former LPGA touring professional Peggy Kirk Bell, the club's owner and resident professional. Its gently sloping hills create constant elevation changes throughout the stretching fairways, and the small, quick greens are a challenging finale to each hole. This inviting course and its charming atmosphere give you a welcome feeling with a generous dose of Pine Needles' Southern hospitality.

Date _____

Score _____

Partners _____

Notes _____

_____

_____

_____

_____

_____

_____

_____

Piñon Hills

*F*rom plateaus to arroyos and stunning wildflowers to rugged brush, Piñon Hills Golf Course offers a diverse desert landscape. Although located in New Mexico, it is situated on the Western Colorado Plateau and provides a glorious view of Colorado's La Plata Mountains. The course itself is a deadly combination of high desert terrain, tiered greens, and thick rough mixed with fescue, rye, and bluegrass. The sixth hole plays over a sandstone canyon and the fifteenth tees off a jutting cliff only to end at a green encircled by jagged rock formations. All things considered, Piñon Hills is not a course for a timid golfer.

Date _____

Score _____

Partners _____

Notes _____

_____

_____

_____

_____

_____

_____

_____

_____

_____

Rifle Creek

*L*ocated on the outskirts of the quaint community of Rifle, Colorado, Rifle Creek Golf Club is surrounded by foothills and farmlands. There are many legends about how the town of Rifle got its name, but the most commonly accepted tells the story of an old trapper who left his rifle leaning against a tree. The town's first settlers discovered the gun years later, weathered and rusted. The Rifle Creek course gives you a sense of the heritage and people of that Rocky Mountain region. Every hole offers a unique vista from sandstone cliffs and the Rocky Mountains to patchwork fields and Rifle Creek itself. The most stunning view comes on the seventh hole where the entire valley spreads out before you, offering its rugged charm.

Date _____

Score _____

Partners _____

Notes _____

_____

_____

_____

_____

_____

_____

_____

Samoset

*H*istory has it that the Pemaquid Indians of the Penobscot Bay area were among the first to greet the Mayflower Pilgrims. Named for the Pemaquid word for "welcome," the luxurious Samoset Resort on the Ocean continues to celebrate this legacy. This welcoming course, situated on a two hundred and thirty-acre peninsula, is a golfer's dream come true. Its refreshing seaside location plays an integral part in Samoset's rigorous golf course. The front nine manages to keep the ocean in view on every hole, and the back nine weaves a trail through gardens, ponds, and woods only to end at the Atlantic. In all, seven holes border the rocky Maine coast. Samoset's signature hole, number seven, dares you to play over the ocean and helped earn the course its nickname—"The Pebble Beach of the East."

Date _____

Score _____

Partners _____

Notes _____

_____

_____

_____

_____

_____

_____

_____

Sandpiper

*S*andpiper Bay Golf and Country Club is one of the many illustrious courses of the Grand Strand. As you might expect in this North Carolina location, lakes and marshes are scattered about the course and its borders are heavily wooded with mature trees. Between the woods, water hazards, and numerous sand traps, the broad fairways allow plenty of room to play. Sandpiper is a haven for golfers and nature lovers alike. In addition to its trademark sandpipers, this lively course features many other wilderness creatures such as deer, herons, alligators, egrets, and eagles.

Date _____

Score _____

Partners _____

Notes _____

_____

_____

_____

_____

_____

_____

_____

_____

_____

Sea Island

The antebellum era comes to life at The Sea Island Golf Club. Located within The Cloister Resort along the southern coast of Georgia, this grand club was founded on the grounds of Retreat Plantation. Many remnants of its days as a working cotton plantation remain, including a slave hospital that is being restored, a corn and fodder barn that now stands in the center of the clubhouse, and a slave graveyard where descendants of former slaves still return to be buried. The four nine-hole golf courses of Sea Island—Plantation, Marshside, Retreat, and Seaside—are as rich in beauty as they are in heritage. Sweeping fairways brightened with bursts of color and surrounded by semitropical vegetation and marshland add the perfect touch to this picture of the Old South.

Date _____

Score _____

Partners _____

Notes _____

_____

_____

_____

_____

_____

_____

_____

_____

Sea Pines

The red-and-white striped lighthouse standing at the end of Harbour Town's eighteenth green is the landmark hole of Sea Pines Plantation on Hilton Head Island. Framed by salt marshes and the water of Calibogue Sound on one side and ancient pines dripping with Spanish moss on the other, it is just as demanding as the other seventeen holes on the Harbour Town course. Sea Pines' Ocean Course features even more water, and the Atlantic wind can carry your ball splashing into it. Although the Sea Marsh course is slightly less taxing than its sister courses, a lagoon borders five of its magnolia-laced holes. This trio of magnificent courses at Sea Pines may be soggy, but their glorious Southern setting makes the experience worthwhile.

Date _____

Score _____

Partners _____

Notes _____

_____

_____

_____

_____

_____

_____

_____

Seaview

arriott's Seaview Resort offers a relaxing escape from the hustle and bustle of nearby Atlantic City. The resort began as a private country club when Donald Ross laid out the Bay Course in 1913. Eventually the Pines Course was developed and Marriott purchased the club, expanded it, and converted it into a resort. Adjacent to New Jersey marshland, the Bay Course is reminiscent of a Scottish links course. The Pines course plays through thick woods brightened by dogwoods and azaleas. Its more than one hundred bunkers and never-ending doglegs make it quite a challenge. Covering 670 acres and overlooking Reeds Bay, Seaview is a sure bet for an enjoyable round of golf.

Date _____

Score _____

Partners _____

Notes _____

_____

_____

_____

_____

_____

_____

_____

_____

Sedona

*S*et against the red rocks of Oak Creek Canyon, The Sedona Golf Resort brings golf and the spirit of the Southwest together. The juniper, oak, pinon, and manzanita painting the rich green foothills of the Coconino National Forest are set dramatically against the shocking red monolithic mesas that tower around the golf course. The course itself presents the natural obstacles of the Arizona desert accented by a surprising variety of waterfalls and lakes. With coyotes, deer, jack rabbits, road runners, and peccaries making occasional appearances, Sedona is unmistakably Southwestern.

Date _____

Score _____

Partners _____

Notes _____

_____

_____

_____

_____

_____

_____

_____

_____

_____

SentryWorld

*L*ocated near the world headquarters of Sentry Insurance in Stevens Point, SentryWorld Golf Course accents its superb golf facilities with natural opulence. Its signature hole alone boasts over ninety thousand plants, including several thousand flowers that explode in radiant color and earn the par-three sixteenth its name, the "Flower Hole." SentryWorld's elegant emerald-green fairways also sparkle with spring-fed lakes and pristine white bunkers in surreal forms. Towering groves of mature trees separate each hole, and dangerous mounds surround their oversized greens. Rocks, streams, and bogs are some of the other natural hazards of the Wisconsin wilderness that both threaten and enhance the scenic SentryWorld course.

Date _____

Score _____

Partners _____

Notes _____

_____

_____

_____

_____

_____

_____

_____

Shangri-La

*N*estled in the northeast corner of Oklahoma, Shangri-La Resort boasts two superior courses and all the natural splendor of the Midwest. Both the Blue and the Gold Courses afford spectacular views of Grand Lake O' the Cherokees from their rolling tree-lined fairways. Forgiving to the novice yet challenging to the seasoned golfer, the Blue Course encounters water on four holes and is marked by oversized, undulating greens. The scenic Gold Course is slightly shorter and more open, bringing water into play on several holes. With the setting sun shining over the glassy surface of Grand Lake, Shangri-La is positively heaven on earth.

Date _____

Score _____

Partners _____

Notes _____

_____

_____

_____

_____

_____

_____

_____

_____

Silverado

*S*ilverado Country Club and Resort, nestled in Napa Valley wine country, offers a truly intoxicating atmosphere. Its North and South Courses will tempt you with the pure beauty of their rolling fairways, sparkling streams and lakes, and majestic oak, redwood, and century-old eucalyptus trees. Overlooking the eighteenth green, the Silverado Mansion now serves as the clubhouse. The land's original owner, Civil War veteran General John Franklin Miller, built the mansion in 1870. A round on either of Silverado's traditional courses is like a relaxing walk through a park—there are no tricks or hidden hazards, and you can see from tee to green on almost every hole. The perfect setting for a round of golf, the Wappo Indians appropriately called the area simply "Talahussi" for "beautiful land."

Date _____

Score _____

Partners _____

Notes _____

_____

_____

_____

_____

_____

_____

Sky Meadow

Golf Digest has rated Sky Meadow Country Club the best golf course in New Hampshire. About a half hour northwest of Boston, Sky Meadow plagues golfers with constant elevation changes that make this target-style course a never-ending challenge. The advantage of its steep hills is one hundred-mile views on cloudless days, but the disadvantage is tricky lies from tee to green. A narrow course with steep inclines, numerous water hazards, and well-bunkered but sizeable greens, Sky Meadow is trying but will keep any stubborn golfer coming back for more.

Date _____

Score _____

Partners _____

Notes _____

_____

_____

_____

_____

_____

_____

_____

_____

_____

_____

Springdale

*N*estled in the woods outside of Ashville, North Carolina, Springdale Country Club is truly a mountain-style golf course. Its sylvan fairways are traversed by sparkling but treacherous streams that have swallowed many a stray golf ball. The view from this rustic locale overlooks the Pisgah National Forest and reaches all the way to the Great Smoky Mountains. Springdale, with its awe-inspiring vistas, is a charming site for a peaceful round of golf.

Date _____

Score _____

Partners _____

Notes _____

_____

_____

_____

_____

_____

_____

_____

_____

_____

_____

Stow Acres

*E*verything about Stow Acres Country Club suggests royal elegance. Commonly considered the best public golf facility in the Boston area, it boasts two superior courses. A magnificent pine forest reigns over the The North Course with trees reaching over one hundred feet high. The older South Course rolls over gentle hills with stately grace. Even the land that Stow Acres lies on has a regal past— it was a gift from the King of England. Stow Acres' proud and prominent courses offer a noble site for a round of golf.

Date _____

Score _____

Partners _____

Notes _____

_____

_____

_____

_____

_____

_____

_____

_____

_____

Sugarbush Inn

*T*he unspoiled perfection of the Mad River Valley is showcased at the Sugarbush Inn Golf Course. Vermont's four thousand-foot high Green Mountains colored by maples, pines, and oaks create a captivating backdrop for golf. The hilly terrain of Sugarbush Inn makes the course as exciting as it is challenging. Perilous drops from elevated tees lead to narrow fairways contoured by the heavily wooded rough, and natural water hazards wait to surprise you at any given turn. Freckled by the lively wildflowers of May or decked in the fiery foliage of fall, this first-class course is a sight to behold anytime of the year.

Date _____

Score _____

Partners _____

Notes _____

_____

_____

_____

_____

_____

_____

_____

_____

_____

_____

Sugarloaf

*S*ettled in the Carrabassett Valley deep in the mountains, Sugarloaf Golf Club is a sublime home for a woodland golf course. Each secluded hole is carved out of the colorful Maine forest and possesses a character all its own. Polished white rocks guide the pristine Carrabassett River as it courses through the back nine, threatening muffed shots. "The String of Pearls," an especially appropriate pseudonym for holes ten through fifteen, glimmers with elegant white birches and crystal clear waters—the signature of Sugarloaf's natural beauty. With breathtaking vistas of the surrounding Longfellow Mountain Range topped off by the occasional moose meeting, Sugarloaf is nothing short of a wilderness adventure.

Date _____

Score _____

Partners _____

Notes _____

_____

_____

_____

_____

_____

_____

_____

Swan Point

*S*kimming the banks of the Potomac River, Swan Point lies just over an hour southeast of Washington, D.C. Its most common hazard, extensive marshlands, makes this swampy course look more befitting to the Carolinas than Maryland. Shaped by over nine hundred acres of great pines and soggy bogs, the elements are an integral part of Bob Cupp's au naturel design. With deer, osprey, heron, and eagle native to the Swan Point area (and Washington not too far off) you'd better keep your eyes peeled—you never know what will creep out of the cattails.

Date _____

Score _____

Partners _____

Notes _____

_____

_____

_____

_____

_____

_____

_____

_____

_____

Tanglewood Park

*T*o fully appreciate Tanglewood Park, you must know its rich history. Before the first settlers arrived in the 1700s, five different Native American tribes thrived on this heavily wooded land. The history continues with William Reynolds who built a twelve hundred-acre farm on the land, which he willed to the town. Today it is the most magnificent public park in North Carolina, featuring two outstanding golf courses: Championship and Reynolds. The Championship course features generous fairways but is made difficult by deep rough and numerous sandy beaches. The Reynolds's fairways are tighter, have noticeably more hills, and feature water as a more prominent hazard. Tanglewood Park has remained virtually untouched over the centuries and a round of golf there is like a trip back in time.

Date _____

Score _____

Partners _____

Notes _____

_____

_____

_____

_____

_____

_____

Temecula Creek

*J*ust northeast of bustling San Diego lies the tranquil Temecula Creek Inn. Its quaint country locale is an ideal spot for its three traditional nine-hole golf courses. The Creek, Oaks, and Stonehouse courses blend flawlessly with their rural environment. They use the variety of native trees, including the sweet-smelling plum and peach, to add difficulty to their rolling layouts. The mountain landscape also plays a part with granite boulders bordering fairways here and there, and the sixty white silica sand traps compensate for the lack of water hazards. From its delicately scented atmosphere to its rustic setting, Temecula Creek Inn embodies the quiet elegance of the game.

Date _____

Score _____

Partners _____

Notes _____

_____

_____

_____

_____

_____

_____

_____

_____

Teton Pines

*A*rnold Palmer and Ed Seay designed the challenging championship course at Teton Pines Golf Club. Located in Jackson, Wyoming, this magnificent golf course surrounds you with natural wonder, including a spectacular view of the Teton Mountain Range. The many streams and lakes wandering throughout the sprawling forty-two acres add difficulty and beauty. The thin air at the course's mountain top locale gives you more power for your punch, carrying the ball about ten percent farther than normal. Teton Pines's wooded setting makes it a bird-watcher's delight with eagles and osprey soaring overhead and sandhill cranes and blue heron perched about the course. But don't spend too much time looking up or a meandering moose may catch you off guard.

Date _____

Score _____

Partners _____

Notes _____

_____

_____

_____

_____

_____

_____

_____

Tiger Point

*S*ituated on Santa Rosa Island off the coast of Pensacola, Tiger Point Golf and Country Club is the jewel of the Emerald Coast. Its East and West Courses uniquely combine a links-style design with tall pines and numerous waterways. Both courses, laid out along the ocean, are waterlogged with lakes, canals, and wetlands. These water features make the Tiger Point courses demanding, but they also bring them to life with egrets poised along the fairways and alligators lurking in the marshes. A golf paradise and a glimpse of the grandeur of native Florida await you at Tiger Point.

Date _____

Score _____

Partners _____

Notes _____

_____

_____

_____

_____

_____

_____

_____

_____

_____

TPC at Sawgrass

*T*he ultimate Pete Dye creation can be found in Ponte Vedra Beach, Florida, at the Sawgrass Resort. Although the resort features seven outstanding courses, it is best known for the TPC Stadium Course. This elegant creation is considered the masterpiece in the Pete Dye gallery. Lush tropical foliage and stately pines accent its meticulously manicured fairways. The Stadium Course's *slightly* milder counterpart, the TPC Valley Course, was also designed by Dye—the fact that it features water on every hole puts the emphasis on "slightly." Between the Stadium and Valley Courses, TPC at Sawgrass is a Pete Dye fan's dream.

Date _____

Score _____

Partners _____

Notes _____

_____

_____

_____

_____

_____

_____

_____

_____

Troon North

*T*he unique desert-links creation of Troon North Golf Club employs the natural contours of the Arizona terrain to imitate an original Scottish links layout. The Sonoran Desert threatens with hazards such as sharp rock outcroppings, deep arroyos, and the prickly saguaro cactus. From elevated tees that provide great views of the surrounding desert to greens set against larger-than-life boulders, this course demands courage as it winds its way around monolithic Pinnacle Peak Mountain. From its innovative design to its unforgettable setting, Troon North is truly one of a kind.

Date _____

Score _____

Partners _____

Notes _____

_____

_____

_____

_____

_____

_____

_____

_____

The Vineyard

*T*his charming golf course derives its name from its location on the site of an old vineyard in Cincinnati. Its gently rolling layout is just challenging enough to provide an enjoyable round of golf without leaving you frustrated. The difficulty of the course increases as you go, and the narrow bluegrass fairways of the back nine become thick with mature trees. Three small lakes dot the course, coming into play on six holes. Although The Vineyard is located on 145 sprawling acres, much of the land surrounding the course is undeveloped in keeping with Hamilton County Parks District's theme, "a space for all species."

Date _____

Score _____

Partners _____

Notes _____

_____

_____

_____

_____

_____

_____

_____

_____

Wintergreen

*T*he dazzling backdrop of the Blue Ridge Mountains and stunning vistas of the Shenandoah Valley are sure to inspire any golfer at the Wintergreen Resort. The resort features two outstanding courses: Devil's Knob and Stoney Creek. Sprawling across 11,000 acres of mountain and valley, Wintergreen's natural features, such as streams and rock outcroppings, chisel a spectacular landscape. A wide variety of trees from sycamores and dogwoods to beeches and pines and an abundance of native wildlife like ducks, deer, and wild geese add even more character to this woodland environment. The deep green forest and misty blue mountains set a picturesque stage for a round of golf, but watch out for the tricky winds they create.

Date _____

Score _____

Partners _____

Notes _____

_____

_____

_____

_____

_____

_____

_____

Notes

Notes

Notes

Notes

Notes

Notes

Photo Credits

All photographs courtesy of the clubs unless otherwise noted.

Anchorage Golf Course (©Ken Graham)

Breckenridge Golf Club (©Bob Winsett)

Cacapon Resort State Park courtesy West Virginia Division of Tourism (©Stephen J. Shaluta Jr.)

Cog Hill Golf and Country Club (©Mike Klemme/Golfoto)

Edgewood Tahoe Golf Club (©Tahoe Foto)

Emerald Valley courtesy Paloma Golf Group, Inc.

Four Seasons Resort and Club (©Mark Humphries)

Montaup Country Club (©Dave Hansen)

Palmas del Mar courtesy Geiger and Associates

Pine Island Golf Club (©Ken Murphy)

Pinon Hills (©Ron Behrmann)

Sea Island Golf Club courtesy Kaufmann and Associates

Sea Pines Plantation (©David S. Soliday)

Sedona Golf Resort (©Tom Johnson)

Shangri-La Resort (©Paul Barton)

Stow Acres (©George N. Peet)

Sugarbush Inn (©Mark Kozlowski)

Sugarloaf Golf Club (©Gary Pearl)

Teton Pines Golf Club (©Dost and Evans Photo)

Tiger Point Golf and Country Club (©Fairways Group)

Troon North Golf Club (©Mike Klemme/Golfoto)

Edgewood Tahoe